D1563711

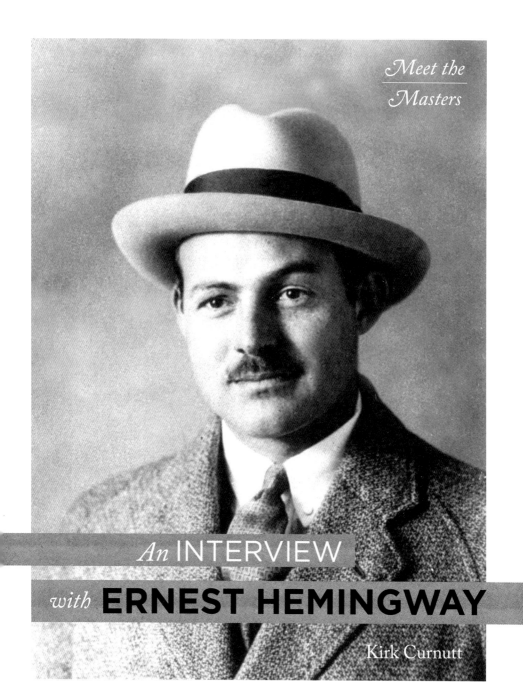

Meet the
Masters

An INTERVIEW

with **ERNEST HEMINGWAY**

Kirk Curnutt

Cavendish
Square

New York

Published in 2015 by Cavendish Square Publishing, LLC
243 5th Avenue, Suite 136, New York, NY 10016

Copyright © 2015 by Cavendish Square Publishing, LLC

First Edition

CPSIA Compliance Information: Batch #WS14CSQ

All websites were available and accurate when this book was sent to press.

Library of Congress Cataloging-in-Publication Data

Curnutt, Kirk, 1964- author.
An interview with Ernest Hemingway / Kirk Curnutt.
pages cm. — (Meet the masters)
Includes index.
ISBN 978-1-62712-915-2 (hardcover) ISBN 978-1-62712-917-6 (ebook)
1. Hemingway, Ernest, 1899-1961. I. Title.
PS3515.E37Z58476 2014
813'.52—dc23
2014002802

Editorial Director: Dean Miller
Senior Editor: Fletcher Doyle
Copy Editor: Michele Suchomel-Casey
Art Director: Jeffrey Talbot

Designer: Amy Greenan
Production Manager: Jennifer Ryder-Talbot
Production Editor: David McNamara
Photo Research: J8 Media

The photographs in this book are used by permission and through the courtesy of: Cover photo, 1, AP Photo/ Charles Scribner Sons; John F. Kennedy Library/File:Ernest Hemingway 1950.jpg/Wikimedia Commons, 4; Jacques Delson/File:LaCloseriedesLilas.jpg/Wikimedia Commons, 8; File:Ernest Hemingway passport photo 40-1548M. jpg/Wikimedia Commons, 9; Lloyd Arnold/File:ErnestHemingway.jpg/Wikimedia Commons, 10; File:Ernest Hemingway with Family, 1905.png/Wikimedia Commons, 13; File:Ernest Hemingway in uniform at Oak Park, Illinois, 1919.jpg/Wikimedia Commons, 16; Hulton Archive/Archive Photos/Getty Images, 19; File:The Hemingway family, Shruns, Austria, 1925.jpg/Wikimedia Commons, 20; John F. Kennedy Presidential Library and Museum/ File:Ernest Hemingway with sons Patrick and Gregory with kittens in Finca Vigia, Cuba.jpg/Wikimedia Commons, 22; File:Gellhorn Hemingway 1941.jpg/Wikimedia Commons, 25; Look Magazine, Photographer/File:Ernest and Mary Hemingway at the Finca Vigia, Cuba - NARA - 192661.jpg/Wikimedia Commons, 28; Earl Theisen Collection/Archive Photos/Getty Images, 30; File:Ernest Hemingway Holding His Son 1927 - NARA - 192694. jpg/Wikimedia Commons, 34–35; File:Ernest Hemingway with sister Marcelline and friends, 1920.jpg/Wikimedia Commons, 37; David E. Scherman/Time & Life Pictures/Getty Images, 38; John F. Kennedy Presidential Library and Museum/File:Ernest Hadley and Bumby Hemingway.jpg/Wikimedia Commons, 41; Carl Van Vechten (1880–1964)/File:Gertrude stein.jpg/Wikimedia Commons, 42; AP Photo, 45; Leonard McCombe/Time & Life Pictures/Getty Images, 46; Gisèle Freund/File:James Joyce with Sylvia Beach at Shakespeare & Co Paris 1920.jpg/ Wikimedia Commons, 49; Topical Press Agency/Hulton Archive/Getty Images, 51; Earl Theisen Collection/Archive Photos/Getty Images, 52; James Burke/Time & Life Pictures/Getty Images, 58; File:Ernest Hemingway with Colonel Charles T. (Buck) Lanham September 18, 1944 - NARA - 192699.jpg/Wikimedia Commons, 60; Lloyd Arnold/Archive Photos/Getty Images, 62–63; Earl Theisen Collection/Archive Photos/Getty Images, 65; Alfred Eisenstaedt/Time & Life Pictures/Getty Images, 66; akg-images/Newscom, 68; Loomis Dean/Time & Life Pictures/ Getty Images, 69; File:Ernest Hemingway Fishing at Walloon Lake, Michigan - NARA - 192667.tif/Wikimedia Commons, 70; Lloyd Arnold/Archive Photos/Getty Images, 73; Mondadori/Getty Images, 74; Hulton Archive/ Getty Images, 77; New York World Telegram and the Sun staff photographer/File:Maxwell Perkins NYWTS. jpg/Wikimedia Commons, 80; Hulton Archive/Archive Photos/Getty Images, 82; akg-images/Newscom, 89; Bob Landry/Time & Life Pictures/Getty Images, 90; Popperfoto/Getty Images, 96; Fotosearch/Archive Photos/Getty Images, 98; Loomis Dean/Time & Life Pictures/Getty Images, 101; Hulton Archive/Getty Images, 103.

CONTENTS

FOREWORD

by John Updike

In the half-century since Ernest Hemingway's shocking suicide by shotgun in 1961, his fame—and did any American writer of the twentieth century enjoy more fame than he?—has attracted denigration from critics and academics who react, perhaps, more to the man's image than his works. He whose hero in *A Farewell to Arms* is a deserter from World War I, and whose portrait of civil war in *For Whom the Bell Tolls* unsparingly reports the atrocities on both sides, is accused of being a lover of violence. His boyhood as a Midwestern doctor's son and his war wounds in Italy at the age of eighteen impressed him with the reality of violence, and his fiction and nonfiction (see *Death in the Afternoon* and his introduction to his anthology *Men at War*) sought to describe this reality, including the hunter's bloodlust; but a fascination is not an endorsement. He is accused of slighting his female characters, yet they— Brett and Catherine and Maria—dominate the canvases of their respective novels, and remain more poignantly, sympathetically, and heroically in the mind than their male lovers do.

Hemingway's apparently simple style, easily parodied, is dismissed as semi-literate when in fact it was a refined and thoughtful product of **modernism** in its youthful prime; he

Ernest Hemingway believed there was a right way to do things, including fishing.

took English prose and, in Ezra Pound's phrase, made it new. The example of modern painting, above all the **scrupulous** post-impressionism of Cézanne, inspired him; newspaper work honed his powers of distillation; wide reading kept his standards elevated. To be sure, he liked a fiesta, and drank too much, but he reported to his writing stand, with freshly sharpened pencils, each dawn; his writing forms a shimmering **paean** to our physical existence, to landscape and weather and healthy senses. His stoic **hedonism** became, in the ruin of conventional pieties left by World War I, a creed for his generation, a laconic lifestyle reflected in popular films, other people's writing, and even common speech.

His first book, published in 1923 in Paris, was titled *Three Stories and Ten Poems*; his short stories, which he effectively stopped producing after collecting them in 1938, are like poems in their concision, polish, and **enigmatic** abruptness. A sense of life's tragic brevity always lies beneath the surfaces of his taut dialogues and evocations of nature. Only the first two novels, *The Sun Also Rises* (1926) and *A Farewell to Arms* (1929), sustain throughout their length the exquisite economy and freshness of the short stories, though the novella *The Old Man and the Sea* (1952) approached their high quality and helped win the author the Nobel Prize in 1954. In his later years, in shaky physical and mental health, he published almost nothing but wrote steadily, accumulating masses of manuscripts that were mined for a number of posthumous publications, of which the most valuable is a fond memoir of his Paris years, *A Moveable Feast* (1964).

The man was a bearish celebrity when literature still bred celebrities; his work remains a touchstone of artistic ardor and luminously clean prose.

INTRODUCTION

More than fifty years after his death, Ernest Hemingway remains arguably the most famous and influential American writer ever. His prominence has not wavered since 1926, when *The Sun Also Rises* made him a symbol of living gracefully amid the upheaval of the post–World War I era. Hemingway continues to inspire because, on the surface at least, he promises us that the line between life's twin compulsions—to work and to play—can be seamless if only we approach every experience with the ethical rigor and exactitude of ritual. Whatever act we might undertake—eating, fishing, loving, boxing, writing—he assures us that there is a right way to do it, and that we can **intuit** that way if we cleanse the moral palate and keep our poise.

With icon status comes oversimplification, however, and the spell Hemingway casts has ensured that his qualities will be distorted to the point of caricature. For every enthusiast who has tried to write in a **Montparnasse** café (I'm guilty of this), fish the Gulf Stream (ditto), or run with the bulls in Pamplona (alas, I lack the necessary *cojones*), there's a resisting reader for whom Hemingway can never connote anything but cartoon **machismo** and **misogyny** and an overheated **stoicism** and **existential** angst. Yet for all the posturing, Hemingway had a keen capacity for knowing when he had dropped the purity of his own line, and he would castigate himself with the same ferocity to which he subjected his rivals during his celebrated literary squabbles.

The cafés of Montparnasse attracted many expatriate writers.

Because the complexities of Hemingway's personality are frequently overlooked, I often find myself imagining interviewing him with the express aim of drawing out his nuances: the self-excoriation of "The Snows of Kilimanjaro," the remorseful nostalgia of *A Moveable Feast*, the wounded idealism of *In Our Time*, and the pragmatic heroism of *For Whom the Bell Tolls*. That's not to leave out the playful pontifications that irked critics of *Death in the Afternoon*, or the often over-the-top muscularity of *To Have and Have Not*, or even the **Rabelaisian** bawdiness of his correspondence. In trying to capture these contradictory voices, the imaginary conversation that follows aspires to return dimensionality to a man whom popular culture has shrouded in truisms and clichés. It also grants him an opportunity to defend himself against modern-day misperceptions. Most of all, this book aims to emphasize the qualities that made him a great writer. With an eye for **le bon mot**, an ear for rhythm, and a talent for saying more with less, Hemingway invigorated literature with an urgency and subtle poignancy that remains as moving in our time as it was in his.

Hemingway's passport photo, circa 1923.

1

ERNEST HEMINGWAY: HIS LIFE IN SHORT

"**H**e wanted to be a great writer," Hemingway says of his alter ego Nick Adams during a contemplative moment in the original draft of "Big Two-Hearted River," the classic 1924 story of a fishing expedition in upper Michigan. "He was pretty sure he would be. He knew it in lots of ways." Although the nine-page meditation in which this admission of ambition appears was eventually deleted, the passage remains intriguing, for it offers an unguarded glimpse of the confidence that convinced the young doctor's son from Oak Park, Illinois, that he was destined for literary eminence. When Hemingway wrote these words, his collected works encompassed only a smattering of sketches and short stories published in obscure **avant-garde** journals and two small, privately printed booklets. By contrast, F. Scott Fitzgerald's debut novel, *This Side of Paradise*, had sold nearly 50,000 copies in 1920, its first year of publication, and his tales of flappers and their starry-eyed beaus were earning outrageous sums from high-circulation **slicks** such as the *Saturday Evening Post*.

Yet barely a year after finishing "Big Two-Hearted River," Hemingway would be hailed as the most original voice of his generation. In addition to "River," several stories in an expanded version of *In Our Time* (1925) proved revolutionary for depicting twentieth-century brutality in frank and uncompromising language. The following year *The Sun Also Rises* made him a youth culture spokesman by inspiring post-collegians galore to repair to expatriate Paris and Pamplona. By the time of his second story collection, *Men Without Women* (1927)—featuring the oft-anthologized "The Killers" and "Hills Like White Elephants"—he was recognized as the originator of a brittle literary minimalism built upon hardboiled bursts of dialogue. Barely thirty when *A Farewell to Arms* was published in 1929, Hemingway was no longer merely an artist but a celebrity, an avatar of adventuresome vitality and sporty manhood. So infectious was his style that other writers had to strive not to sound like him. His popular audience, meanwhile, lived vicariously through what the press trumpeted as his glamorous globetrotting.

One thing often overlooked within the larger outline of Hemingway's biography is the importance of his work ethic. "First there must be talent," he argues in *Green Hills of Africa* (1935). "Then there must be discipline … Then there must be the conception of what it can be and an absolute conscience as unchanging as the standard meter in Paris, to prevent faking."

This "absolute conscience" was largely the legacy of his father, Clarence Edmonds Hemingway (1871–1928), a respected though not prominent general practitioner whose gruff and stolid reputation reflected his **abhorrence** of loafing. Even at the family's summer home on Walloon Lake near Petoskey, Michigan, the father insisted that his six children adopt a devoutly ethical approach to recreation. The hunting, camping, and fishing that Ernest grew up learning were not diversions but self-improving moral exercises. Clarence's Victorian belief in self-regulation and self-improvement imbued Hemingway with a seriousness of purpose that would reverberate in his descriptions of even the simplest of leisure activities. The stern professionalism of his **ethos** likewise reflects Clarence's

The Hemingway family, left to right: Marcelline, Sunny, C.E. Hemingway, Grace Hemingway, Ursula, and Ernest.

rectitude. The disparaging judgments that he would level against his peers echo the admonitions against indolence that he grew up hearing from his father.

The other pronounced aspect of Hemingway's personality, his penchant for showmanship, was inherited from his mother, Grace Hall Hemingway (1872–1951), an amateur contralto and painter. Although Hemingway came to loathe his mother—blaming her overbearingness for the harrowing depressions that Clarence suffered—his charisma and restless enthusiasm came from her. Later biographers such as Kenneth Lynn have depicted Grace as emasculating Ernest, first by dressing him and his older sister, Marcelline (1898–1963), as androgynous identical twins in their childhood, and later by inveigling him into a "deliciously intimate dependency" by disapproving of the very unapologetic individuality she had **bequeathed** him. Yet Mrs. Hemingway was hardly an overbearing or domineering mother. She was, rather, like many artists, a little self-preoccupied—a trait her son would also absorb. As with many Victorian-bred parents, she was also ill-prepared to deal with the generation gap separating her from her modern-minded son, an inability that sometimes rendered her incapable of appreciating his literary accomplishments—in 1951 she told a Detroit newspaper that she considered Ernest's schoolboy essays to be better than his books. For all the praise he received throughout his career, Hemingway could never quite overcome such disapproval. "She hates my guts," he complained around the time of that interview, which infuriated him so much he threatened to cut off financial support.

However much Hemingway's personality was shaped by his oddly paired parents, his writing could not have developed as it did had he not left the conservative environs of Oak Park after graduating from high school in 1917. A series of formative experiences began to shape his sensibility. Eschewing college, he worked as a cub reporter for the *Kansas City Star*, whose style sheet offered "the best rules I ever learned for the business of writing." Later collected as *Ernest Hemingway: Cub Reporter* (1970), the dozen or so unsigned pieces produced during his tenure reveal the influence of *Star* dos and don'ts, such as "Use short sentences" and "Avoid the use of adjectives." They also introduce his fascination with the seamy underside of crime, whose gangsters and gunmen would reappear in "The Killers" and his most noirish novel, *To Have and Have Not* (1937).

Even more decisive was Hemingway's service as an ambulance driver for the American Red Cross in Italy in mid-1918. Like many young men his age, Ernest was eager to see combat after the United States entered the Great War in November 1917. He had grown up hearing stories of both of his grandfathers' exploits during the American Civil War and imagined himself carrying on their heroism. Yet poor eyesight prevented him from enlisting, and he went abroad as a relief worker rather than a soldier. Less than a month into his service, on July 8, 1918, he was seriously wounded in a mortar attack along the Piave River near the city of Fossalta, his legs and groin riddled with shrapnel. The wounding became the formative event of his career. Both his terror and the heroism credited to him (he was awarded an Italian medal of valor for tending to Italian soldiers caught in the same attack) form the central motifs of *In Our Time*, *A Farewell to Arms*, and several stories.

His subsequent recuperation at the Red Cross Hospital in Milan introduced him to a second integral theme. While there he fell in love with an American nurse, Agnes von Kurowsky (1892–1984). Yet two months after he returned to Oak Park in January 1919, she informed him that their courtship was over, even though Ernest was telling his friends that they were engaged. Love and war were thus inexorably mingled in Hemingway's mind, with both *A Farewell to Arms* and *For Whom the Bell Tolls* (1940) bitterly insisting that, in a world rife with the latter, the former cannot provide any escape from pain.

Ernest Hemingway spent part of his recovery at his parents' home in Oak Park, Illinois.

The third formative experience didn't occur until December 1921, when Hemingway expatriated to Paris at the suggestion of author Sherwood Anderson (1876–1941) to join the burgeoning modern arts movement. By that time he was newly married to Hadley Richardson (1891–1979),

whom he'd met in Chicago while freelancing for the
Toronto Daily Star. Despite Hemingway's war experience,
early attempts at fictionalizing it were no more than pale
imitations of the Rudyard Kipling adventures he'd read as a
boy. As Anderson promised, the American colony in Paris
was revolutionizing literature, inventing new methods for
conveying the uncertain temper of the times. Accordingly,
once in Paris, the Hemingways ingratiated themselves with
modernist luminaries such as Gertrude Stein (1873–1946)
and Ezra Pound (1885–1972). Absorbing the heady
atmosphere that was producing such landmarks as James
Joyce's *Ulysses* (1922), Hemingway quickly found his
voice through painstaking writing exercises he developed
for himself, despite the necessity of posting stories for
the *Star*, for which he served as a foreign correspondent
through 1923. Hemingway learned from Stein how to
vary his sentences through rhythm and repetition. He also
assimilated her ideas on description, a subject she lectured
on while showing off her impressive collection of paintings
by Paul Cézanne, Henri Matisse, and Pablo Picasso. While
Pound introduced him to experimental techniques that
pared his sentences down to imagistic fragments, his main
influence was as a patron: it was thanks to Pound that 300
copies of *Three Stories and Ten Poems* were printed in 1923,
officially inaugurating Hemingway's literary career.

   That same year, at the invitation of the avant-garde
journal *Little Review*, the author produced a sextet of violent
vignettes involving war and bullfighting (to which Stein
had introduced him). **Viscerally** immediate, the pieces were
so sparsely worded that Hemingway called his technique
"unwriting." Along with a subsequent dozen fragments, these
"postcards from hell," as one critic describes them, formed

the basis of *In Our Time*, a 170-copy collection published by friend and fellow journalist William Bird's Three Mountains Press. The small volume won Hemingway his first critical acclaim, with Edmund Wilson (1895–1972) proclaiming, "I am inclined to think that this little book has more artistic dignity than any other that has been written by an American about the period of the war."

The year 1924 was to be Hemingway's ***annus mirabilis***, seeing the writing and/or publication of several influential stories that defined his major themes: the quest to establish one's place in nature ("Big Two-Hearted River"); initiation into a knowledge of death and violence ("Indian Camp"); the war generation's estrangement from Victorian values ("Soldier's Home"); and alienation and the impermanence of love ("Out of Season" and "Cat in the Rain," both of which equate marital instability with expatriate isolation). Hemingway's aptitude for networking and attracting publicity likewise elevated his reputation. By the time a commercial version of *In Our Time* appeared in 1925 from the New York publisher Boni & Liveright, many peers and aspiring writers were seeking him out as he previously had Stein and Pound.

In April 1925, he accidentally encountered F. Scott Fitzgerald (1896–1940) in the Dingo Bar, Paris, two weeks after the publication of *The Great Gatsby*. Fitzgerald would be instrumental in finessing his friend's relationship with editor Maxwell Perkins at Charles Scribner's Sons, which would become Hemingway's exclusive publisher starting with the satire *The Torrents of Spring* (1926).

Six weeks after meeting Fitzgerald, Ernest and Hadley departed for Hemingway's third trip to the San Fermín bullfighting festival in Pamplona, Spain. Thanks to a rowdy

F. Scott Fitzgerald
had similar
roots to Ernest
Hemingway's.

entourage of fellow expatriates, the trip was muddled with
sexual jealousy and drunken fistfights, most inspired by
a dissolute divorcée named Duff Twysden (1893–1938).
Both intrigued and repulsed by Duff's disaffected lifestyle,
Hemingway shortly transformed the trip into a *roman-à-
clef*-cum-generational fable about postwar disillusionment.
Originally titled *The Lost Generation* (a phrase borrowed from
Stein), *The Sun Also Rises* became a youth-cult phenomenon.
Journalist Jake Barnes's inability to love the promiscuous
Brett Ashley because of a debilitating war injury that
renders him impotent symbolized his generation's belief
that it lacked the ability to engage fully with life. Thanks
in no small part to *The Sun*'s reputation as a guidebook to
expatriate Paris, the novel became a *succès de scandale*, and

Ernest, Hadley, and Jack "Bumby" Hemingway enjoy the snow and sun in Schruns, Austria.

Hemingway quickly supplanted Fitzgerald as the reigning spokesman for the under-thirty set.

In contrast to this success, Hemingway's private life was in turmoil. In late 1926 he left Hadley and their son, John or "Bumby" (b. 1923), for Pauline Pfeiffer (1895–1951), a *Paris Vogue* staffer who'd recently joined the Hemingways' expatriate circle. Later, in *A Moveable Feast*, Hemingway would equate the end of his first marriage with the loss of his artistic purity. At the time, however, he was drawn to Pauline, the daughter of a prosperous entrepreneur from Piggott, Arkansas, because she was both worldlier and wealthier than the shy, sheltered Hadley. Ernest and Pauline married in April 1927 and returned to the United States in 1928, settling in Key West, Florida, which would become their base for the next decade. Drawing upon his war experience, Hemingway was by then into a second novel about another American wounded by war, this time a lieutenant in the Italian army, who falls in love with his Red Cross nurse. Work was interrupted in late 1928 by an event that would haunt his future fiction: on December 6, Clarence Hemingway killed himself with the same .32 caliber pistol that Ernest's revered grandfather, Anson, had carried during the Civil War. For three decades to come, Hemingway would grapple with the specter of his father's death, fending off his own "black ass" depressions while trying to decide whether suicide was heroic or cowardly.

Upon publication in September 1929, *A Farewell to Arms* was hailed as the quintessential World War I novel, thanks to Hemingway's gripping depiction of the Italian army's 1917 retreat from Caporetto, where they were routed by Austrian troops.

"I was always embarrassed by the words sacred, glorious, and sacrifice," thinks Frederic Henry the night before the disastrous battle. "I had seen nothing sacred, and the things that were glorious had no glory and the sacrifices were like the stockyards at Chicago if nothing was done with the meat except to bury it."

A grim if sometimes melodramatic tragedy, in which Lieutenant Henry deserts the war to retrieve Catherine Barkley, only to lose her and their stillborn child to a botched Caesarean section, *Farewell* introduced Hemingway to a much wider popular audience than *In Our Time* or even *The Sun Also Rises*—selling nearly 30,000 copies in its first month despite the near-simultaneous onslaught of the Great Depression. The novel also cemented his reputation as a consummate craftsman. Thanks to a breathless *New Yorker* profile by Dorothy Parker (1893–1967), Hemingway became known for the dedicated hard work and sheer effort

Papa plays with sons Patrick and Gregory and their cats at La Finca Vigía, his estate in Cuba.

that he put into his art. As "proof," Parker told the story of how Hemingway rewrote the ending of *Farewell* seventy times—which was only a slight exaggeration (it was actually twenty-eight times).

Despite *Farewell*'s success—or perhaps because of it—almost a decade would pass before Hemingway completed another book-length fiction. Instead, the 1930s marked the emergence of his "Papa" persona, the querulous, often hectoring grand master of American letters who might produce a short-story classic such as "A Clean, Well-Lighted Place" (1933) when not trawling the Gulf of Mexico in his custom fishing boat, the *Pilar*, hunting kudu on the Serengeti, or posing for magazine photos with his boys (a third son, Gregory, was born in 1931). Yet popular misperceptions of this era do a severe disservice to the nonfiction to which the author now devoted his attention. While reviewers panned both *Death in the Afternoon* (1932) and *Green Hills of Africa* (1935), these books are nevertheless fascinating for their mixture of styles, voices, and genres—all tightly regulated by a ritualistic regard for the morality of sport. The former finds Hemingway drawing constant parallels between bullfighting and writing as he defines artistic standards of authenticity.

The latter, a record of Ernest and Pauline's 1933–34 African safari, offers some of his richest descriptions of landscape. In between these efforts, Hemingway became a regular contributor to *Esquire*, a new men's magazine that mingled fashion and fiction. His dispatches from Cuba, Key West, and Africa provide insight into the author's politics, his notions of masculinity, and his irritation at his own celebrity. This period marked a severe reassessment of his literary merits. When his story collection *Winner Take Nothing* appeared in 1933, reviewers complained that such efforts as "Wine of Wyoming" and "The Gambler, the Nun, and the Radio" suggested "a lack of growth" and a "monotonous repetition of subjects … eating and drinking, travel, sport, coition." Unfortunately, *To Have and Have Not*, Hemingway's first novel since *A Farewell to Arms*, did little to reverse this opinion. In drafting the novel, the author even referenced his own decline, with one character bicycling past the Hemingways' home at 907 Whitehead Street to note how the "big slob" living there had failed his promise.

Although Hemingway deleted this scene from his final version, he did allow one stunning example of self-repudiation into print. In his greatest short story, "The Snows of Kilimanjaro" (1936), a writer dying from gangrene while on safari in Africa must admit to having squandered his talent through drinking and womanizing. All the memories Harry Walden has failed to transform into fiction come back to haunt him in the form of lyrical interior monologues that convey Hemingway's remorseful nostalgia for the heyday of 1920s Paris. Although the story takes rather ungenerous swipes at Pauline and Fitzgerald, there's no doubt that Hemingway is the real target of his own irate disappointment.

Despite "Snows," the inspiration for Hemingway's artistic renaissance was not his personal regrets but the international scene. In 1937, he traveled to Spain to cover the civil war that erupted when totalitarian troops under aspiring dictator Francisco Franco attempted to unseat the country's fledgling Republican government. Devoutly anti-Fascist, Hemingway lent his credibility and celebrity to the leftist cause, helping to produce a propagandistic documentary, *The Spanish Earth*, while working as a correspondent for the North American News Alliance. After four separate tours of Spain in 1937–38, Hemingway realized that the cause was doomed, and he retreated to Key West to weigh the value of political commitment in a world of corrupted ideologies. The result was *For Whom the Bell Tolls*, which, despite some stilted stream-of-consciousness interludes, many still regard as Hemingway's greatest novel. As with *A Farewell to Arms*, an impossible love story unfolds across the backdrop of war, with the American munitions expert Robert Jordan seeking to save a brutalized woman, Maria. Populated with colorful characters, *For Whom* echoed the message of *In Our Time* by insisting that the separate peace of personal integrity is the only reliable measure of morality when the fog of war makes heroes and villains indistinguishable. Thanks to its timeliness (the book appeared at the onset of World War II), it became Hemingway's greatest success yet, selling nearly 500,000 copies within its first six months.

As during the publication of *A Farewell to Arms*, Hemingway's private life was in turmoil, and yet another decade would pass before he again completed a book, much less a novel. In December 1936, he met the writer Martha Gellhorn (1908–1998), and their affair during the Spanish

Martha Gellhorn, a dedicated journalist, joined Hemingway on a trip to Chungking, China, in 1941.

Civil War spelled the end for his second marriage. Ernest and Pauline were divorced in late 1940, by which point Hemingway and Gellhorn were living together at a Cuban estate called La Finca Vigía, making annual expeditions to Sun Valley, Idaho. Hemingway's third marriage was his shortest and unhappiest. Unaccustomed to a wife as devoted to her career as he was to his, he resented Martha's frequent absences on journalism assignments.

After the Japanese attack on Pearl Harbor in December 1941, Hemingway sought to assist in the war effort by patrolling the Gulf for German submarines. In 1944, eager to see the European front, he finagled press credentials from *Collier's* magazine (for which Gellhorn also worked) and covered the Allied landing on D-Day, before accompanying the Royal Air Force on bombing missions. He participated in the liberation of Paris and the Hürtgenwald Forest drive into Germany, eventually being called before the army inspector general for acting as a combatant rather than a correspondent.

In London, shortly before D-Day, Hemingway met journalist Mary Welsh (1908–1986), with whom he entered yet another extramarital relationship. Divorce from Gellhorn ensued, and the couple married in 1946, settling at La Finca Vigía, where Hemingway began a pair of projects that would not be read publicly until after his death: *Islands in the Stream* (1970) and *The Garden of Eden* (1986). When a new novel called *Across the River and Into the Trees* did finally appear in 1950, its May–December romance plot (based on the author's flirtation with an Italian teenager named Adriana Ivancich) was widely panned. Two years later, Hemingway rebounded with *The Old Man and the Sea*, a deceptively simple man-versus-nature story in which a poor Cuban fisherman, Santiago, loses a 1,000-pound (450 kilogram) marlin to marauding sharks. The book led to Hemingway's winning two prizes he had long coveted: the Pulitzer in 1953 and the Nobel in 1954.

Unlike most recipients of literature's most prestigious honor, Hemingway did not travel to Stockholm to address the Swedish Academy. His health was too poor. Only in his mid-fifties, he looked two decades older, thanks to alcoholism, hypertension, and the ravages of not one but two plane crashes survived on consecutive days in Africa. Besieged by reporters, he spent much of 1954–55 trying to avoid publicity hounds in order to work on a semifictional account of the African safari that had occasioned the crashes. After years of being encouraged to write his autobiography, he started recording memories of expatriate Paris in 1956. Posthumously published as *A Moveable Feast* (1964), the sketches find Hemingway once again preaching his credo of disciplined artistry while offering unflattering vignettes of Stein, Fitzgerald, and other writers who failed his standards. Yet he saves his harshest judgments for himself, obliquely regretting the loss of his first wife and his corruption at the hands of flattering friends.

Hemingway had envisioned publishing his memoirs in 1960, followed by an update of *Death in the Afternoon* that would include an account of the spectacular 1959 bullfighting season. However, poor health, depression, and paranoia intervened. The Castro revolution forced Ernest and Mary from La Finca Vigía, and Hemingway grew convinced that the FBI was monitoring his activities—a concern that has since been substantiated. J. Edgar Hoover was indeed informed when, at Mary's insistence, Hemingway entered the Mayo Clinic in late 1960. (Hoover's interest was likely spurred by pro-Castro statements Hemingway made.) The electroshock therapy received there exacerbated Ernest's condition, obliterating his memory and rendering him incapable of writing. Nevertheless, after two suicide attempts

Mary Welsh was married to Hemingway longer than any of his other three wives.

in April 1961, he returned to the clinic for additional treatments. Convincing his doctors he was cured, he was released in late June and returned to Ketchum, Idaho, where he and Mary owned a home.

There, on the morning of July 2, only two days after his arrival, he killed himself with his favorite 12-gauge Boss shotgun.

"I want to run as a writer," Hemingway wrote in a 1950 letter. "Not as a man who had been to wars; nor a bar room fighter; nor a shooter; nor a horse-player; nor a drinker. I would like to be a straight writer and be judged as such … " Since his death, admirers have not always honored this request. On any given day you can find them in Paris, Pamplona, Oak Park, Petoskey, Key West, Ketchum, and many other places searching for traces of the personality that saturates his every sentence. What was Hemingway really like, they want to know. The fact that new biographies, memoirs, and academic studies continue to appear year after year suggests just how elusive the answer truly is.

2

ERNIE AGONISTES

Hemingway no sooner achieved a measure of renown than his personality changed: gone was the sensitive, aspiring writer known variously as Hem, Wemedge, and Tatie, to be replaced by a belligerent figure who lashed out at critics and impetuously broke with friends. As Gertrude Stein said, Hemingway seemed at war with himself, his burly **truculence** becoming "a disguise for the thing that was really gentle and fine in him." As a result, discerning readers have sought to understand why a writer so capable of capturing emotional nuance allowed himself, in the words of Edmund Wilson, to become "his own worst-drawn character."

Q. Sorry, I don't mean to interrupt while you're working, but I need some advice. I have a war story I want to write. I was hoping you might help me. Nobody writes a better war story than you.

You can punk off if you came here to flatter me. That's not why I work—you think I whittle sentences down to the truest words possible so somebody who talks like he's constipated will admire me? There's a café called the Rotonde up the street. You'll get your money's worth of advice there. Advice from artists is the cheapest thing on the menu.

Hemingway used boxing to stay fit, even during a trip to Kenya.

Q. When you get this strident, it really saddens me. You can't convince me that someone who writes a sentence as beautiful as this one is as hardboiled as you pretend to be: "When I saw my wife again standing by the tracks as the train came in by the piled logs at the station, I wish I had died before I ever loved anyone but her." When you go all bellicose it just seems … insincere. It makes your admirers wonder what happened to you.

Oh, nerts. You're going to be like all the rest, aren't you? You're going to tell me how much I've influenced you, and then you're going to turn around and tell me all the ways I've failed you. You'll knock me for being famous, say my women characters are flat and unrealistic male fantasies, and then tell me my style was so original I ended up parodying myself. Then you'll let me know exactly when my train went off its tracks. Go ahead. You won't be the first.

Q. You're very defensive, as you usually were with the press and public. Why is that?

Listen, I come from a time when the writing was supposed to be more important than the writer. That was the idea behind the movement I was part of. In modernism you take yourself out of the work so the reader experiences your words, not you. Writing's supposed to be about the art, but most readers only care about personality.

Q. Aren't you a bit to blame for that? Your fiction is so transparently autobiographical that readers are naturally intrigued by the life that inspired it.

The only writing that's any good is what you make up, out of your imagination. That's what makes things ring true. Good writing has truths that aren't necessarily facts. You do understand the difference between truths and facts, don't you? Maybe if you did, you wouldn't accuse me of going phony.

Q. You've certainly had to deal with plenty of half-truths. Is there one particular misperception that irritated you?

Definitely the war. Here's the gen. Papa went to war and got blown up on the Italian front. A few years later Papa went to write about getting blown up, only for dramatic purposes he made his people soldiers instead of ambulance drivers. Papa never claimed to be a soldier, but the newspapers decided he must've been to write so swell about war. That thing you gentlemen just tossed out with baby and bathwater both? It's called dramatic license.

Q. It's not that simple, is it? I mean, please don't punch me—but biographers have shown how when you came home from the war you told different versions of what happened to you there. Sometimes you boasted that you carried another man on your back, sometimes that you bravely told doctors to tend to other wounded first. Once you claimed you threw away your revolver so you wouldn't be tempted to shoot yourself.

That mortar didn't care whether I was a combatant or a canteen boy when it came at me. I've got 227 scars to prove it. As for all that other stuff … OK, so I gilded a little lily at first. But I never fudged facts after I became a writer.

Q. Did you try to correct some of those legends that sprouted up around you?

I spent years clearing up the biographical hooey when I should've been writing. When *The Sun Also Rises* came out,

Hemingway—seen here with his son Bumby—hated biographical material.

my publisher ruined a portrait of me by John Blomshield by trying to fertilize said portrait with a load of biographical crap. The portrait was very fine but the crap stank. Not only did they say I was in the Italian infantry—they said I was a football star and that I fought my way through college as a boxing instructor. Not only was I never a boxing instructor, Christ knows I never went to college!

Maybe it was my fault. I didn't give Scribner's any facts my first time out, so they had to work with what they'd heard about me. I was naïve in thinking biography was as unimportant to readers as it was to me. Hell, the same thing happened when they made the first movie version of *A Farewell to Arms* in '32. The Hollywood flacks put out so much horse manure about me, it's a wonder the horse didn't die of dysentery. I had to issue a press release: "Mr. H. appreciates the publicity attempt to build him into a glamorous personality like Floyd Gibbons or Tom Mix's horse Tony but he deprecates it and asks the motion picture people to leave his private life alone."

Q. Clearly, you don't like biography. Why not?

Nothing kills the fiction faster than psychoanalyzing the writer. It's invasive and destructive. It's like in the early

'50s, when all the professors came after me. They were a nightmare combination of junior-G men, **Rorschach** testers from the Herr Sigmund school, and Kremlin keyhole-peepers. Most weren't professing—they were pursuing.

Q. Things haven't changed much, then. It seems that with every new biography there's a new angle on the very thing you say readers are too fixated on—your personality.

Biographing besieges a guy—it's invasive and inhibiting. You try putting new words to paper when you've got a school of interpretation out there saying everything you write about can be traced back to your taking shrapnel in your Balzac in a war. You try it when you've got fools saying you wasted your talent proving your manhood because your mother dressed you like your sister when you were a baby. You do that when everybody you ever drank or shot pheasant or baited tackle with has written a memoir diagnosing your neuroses …

Q. So how would you respond to people like Gertrude Stein, who said readers would discover a very different Hemingway if you ever exposed your real self?

I'd borrow a line from "Hills Like White Elephants" and say, "Would you please please please please please please stop talking?" Papa is many people, just like you are many people, dear reader, and personality is a hell of a dull talk. What's important is the work.

Friends gather with Marcelline and Ernest Hemingway, third and second from right, near the family vacation spot on Lake Petoskey in Michigan.

Q. If I promise not to psychoanalyze and stick to the writing, may I join you?

All right. Pull up a chair and order a *distingué* and *cervelas* with a plate of *pommes à l'huile*. By the time they get here you'll have an opening line for your war story—if you're serious about writing.

While you're making yourself comfortable, I'm going to give you a nickname. I love nicknames—I give one to everybody who comes my way. If I don't think I like you I'll call you something belittling.

And if I don't dislike you, I'll call you something that's only affectionately belittling, just so you remember who's Papa. From here on out, you'll answer to Maestro, and we'll decide at the end of these interviews just which of those categories you fall into.

3

ON WAR

Hemingway was one of the first writers to depict the dehumanizing psychological effects of combat. Yet war was more than simply his initiation into brutality. In a 1942 anthology he edited, *Men at War*, he described how diametrically opposite the arts of soldiering and writing really are. Whereas the former requires one to live in the moment "with no before and no after," the latter requires suspending disbelief—an imaginative faculty that can get a man killed on the battlefield. Ultimately, Hemingway's interest in war exposes his anxieties about the role of imagination in writing and the place of fiction in everyday life.

Q. OK, so the story I want to write is about a war that's been going on so long people are inured to it. The casualty count goes up every day, but the home front has tuned it out. They're more concerned with celebrity gossip.

Stop right there. Your story's already been written. It's called "In Another Country." I wrote it in 1927, and you won't top it. You might think you can knock me out of the ring, but you won't. I KO'd all the war-story boys with "In Another Country." Crane?—right hook. Stendhal?—left. Tolstoy?—uppercut.

Becoming a correspondent was the only way Hemingway could get close to World War II.

Q. Oh, yes. I know what you mean—"In Another Country" may be the most underappreciated of your masterpieces. That opening sentence! "In the fall the war was always there, but we did not go to it any more." Fitzgerald said it was one of the most beautiful prose sentences he'd ever read. That's what I love about that story, and other ones with Nick Adams, such as "Now I Lay Me" and "A Way You'll Never Be." There's a cathartic fragility in them. It's typical of the crushing vulnerability of your best work. You're right—I won't top it.

No, and you won't even get into the fight if you keep lunging at me with that many syllables. Cathartic fragility? Crushing vulnerability? Cripes. Maybe I should have nicknamed you Faulkner instead of Maestro. Lay off the adjectives, will you?

Q. Let's say I was heading to war. What would it teach me about writing?

War's such a great experience for a writer because, as I once wrote, "it groups the maximum of material and speeds up the action and brings out all sorts of stuff that you normally have to wait a lifetime to get."

Q. What "stuff"?

You know what, I may just have to shorten your nickname from Maestro to Mice—you seem a little mousy to me. The meaning's right there for you.

Read *In Our Time*. Not all of its vignettes are war scenes, but many are, and each captures a little sliver of experience in a way that's intense and immediate. Among others, you have a kitchen corporal accompanying a battery to Champagne, a soldier "potting" Germans as they come over a garden wall in Mons, the contrast between another soldier's fear while under bombardment and his unwillingness to admit that terror the next night while romping with a whore.

I called these fragments "unwritten stories," because in them there's only a minimum of context—no sense of what has happened or what will come, only that second of experience in its purity. You don't need the before or after because the present's all there—crystalline and transparent, but not, as the college boys like to think, shallow.

Q. I see the "unwritten" quality in your stories because they're so compact. What about your novels, though? Doesn't a full-length plot demand some before and after? How did you balance the visceral immediacy of war against the need to advance the action in *A Farewell to Arms* or *For Whom the Bell Tolls*?

Hemingway regretted leaving his first wife, Hadley.

It wasn't easy. It took me ten years after I was blown up to do *Arms*. I tried a couple of times before that. Around the time I married Hash—that's what I used to call Hadley, my first wife—I was trying to make something out of the war, but

Gertrude Stein provided constructive criticism and valuable lessons to a young Hemingway.

I couldn't find the structure. I thought about jumbling some fragments together like Scott Fitzgerald did in *This Side of Paradise* but, thank Christ, Mrs. Hemingstein (Hemingstein being a nickname I gave myself as kid) talked me out of that. She did, and so did Gertrude—Miss Stein told me there was too much description and it was lousy to boot and that I should start over. So I did.

Q. One of your main legacies is the psychological duress of combat that you depict in stories like "In Another Country," "Now I Lay Me," and "A Way You'll Never Be." People today take post-traumatic stress disorder for granted, but in the 1920s the concept of "shell shock" was new.

Even though those stories were invented, I knew that stress personally. "In Another Country" was me recuperating in Milan in 1918 with my knee all shot to strudel with a medal I wasn't sure I deserved, and unable to sleep. Did I really lie, as I wrote, "in bed by myself at night, afraid to die and wondering how I would be when I went back to the front again"? Of course I did. Maybe not all the time. There were happy things in Milan, like me and Agnes von Kurowsky, who became the nurse in *A Farewell to Arms*—but those weren't important to that story.

"Now I Lay Me" was about going back to the war, which I never did but I could have, you see, and it was how I knew I would've felt because I was already feeling that way. By '27, when I was writing both those stories, I really had "been living for a long time with the knowledge that if I ever shut my eyes in the dark and let myself go, my soul would go out of my body," as I wrote in "Now I Lay Me." I'd been that way for a long time ever since I'd been blown up at night and felt it go out of me and go off and then come back.

So, you see, you have to write about what you know, not what you've studied, and if you haven't seen the bloat of the dead with their pockets pulled out and gone through and all the paper that rains down after a shelling—there's always as much paper as rubble—you've got no business writing about it.

From the look of you, I doubt you've been anywhere near a war. Maybe you should try the Dingo instead of the Rotonde. That might be more your crowd.

Q. I'll ignore the insinuation and simply point out how brilliantly you also depict survivor's guilt.

I did it best in "Soldier's Home." It's about the guilt of telling people the war stories they want to hear: "Harold Krebs felt the need to talk but no one wanted to hear about it. His town had heard too many atrocity stories to be thrilled by actualities. Krebs found that to be listened to at all he had to lie … A distaste for everything that had happened to him in the war set in because of the lies he had told."

Q. So what is the major theme of your war writing? It seems contradictory. The message of *A Farewell to Arms* is almost diametrically opposed to that of *For Whom the Bell Tolls*. The first says war is inhumane, but the second says we can find our humanity through it.

There are many themes in my war work because war never means just one thing. *In Our Time* was existential before existential existed. In one vignette Nick Adams tells a fellow wounded soldier named Rinaldi that if they can survive they'll each have made their own peace. That was my way of saying that the so-called Great War left those of us who'd been there looking for some individual beachhead of dignity amid the killing fields of existence.

Arms was grimmer. At college they'll teach you to classify it as naturalism. I was saying that what war can't break in you, life will. That's why at the end Catherine and her baby die in childbirth. If they didn't, none of the death that Frederic Henry sees in battle would mean anything—he'd think he could escape it. As I wrote in *Death in the Afternoon*, "All stories, if continued far enough, end in death, and he is no true storyteller who would keep that from you."

For Whom the Bell Tolls was different because that was a different war. I was saying there's real conviction to be had even when what you believe in is being corrupted. Robert Jordan recognizes that and accepts his death. Even if his side will lose the Spanish Civil War, even if the Communists backing his side are as murderous as the Fascists they're fighting, his death is not a waste because he's done his duty with integrity. He's upheld his ideals.

Q. It's worth pointing out how influential your war fiction was outside of literary circles. Generals and

Fidel Castro learned tactics of war by reading Hemingway.

grunts alike read you. Politicians, too. It's hard to imagine today's policymakers looking to novels and stories for moral insights into combat.

You're right, but literature back then had real consequences. It wasn't just something to dissertate on. You know who used *For Whom the Bell Tolls* as a manual on guerrilla warfare? None other than Fidel Castro. That book was all the formal training he had for overthrowing Batista in Cuba in 1959. Of course, I might've been more flattered if his *coup* hadn't cost me my favorite house, not to mention a country I loved. *Viva la revolución*, indeed!

4

ON EXPATRIATION

T he success of *The Sun Also Rises* in 1926 helped popularize the phenomenon of expatriation, inspiring young Americans to live abroad, whether in Paris, on the Riviera, in Italy, or in Spain. A 1928 *Harper's* essay, "Babes in the Bois," speaks of the novel's influence on the postwar generation: "Youngsters learned it by heart and ... immediately took a ship for Paris to be the disciples of the new faith of disaffection ..." Hemingway resented his reputation as spokesman for "the Lost Generation," even though *The Sun Also Rises* popularized that term. As he always insisted, some may have gone to Paris for the drink and debauchery, but he went to work.

Q. It's amazing to see the difference between your juvenilia and what you accomplished shortly after arriving in Paris in December 1921. What does expatriation teach a writer?

It teaches you dislocation, which sharpens the memory and makes you able to recall details you take for granted when you're in the actual place you're writing about. In *A Moveable Feast* I called it "transplanting yourself," and I said it's "as necessary with people as with other sorts of growing things."

Hemingway won the Nobel Prize for Literature about the time this photo was taken in 1954.

Here's a little secret: if you want to judge my best stuff, look for things that aren't set where I was when I wrote them.

Q. Like your Michigan stories? If I tried to write something like "Big Two-Hearted River," I think I'd need to be in the Upper Peninsula, walking through the burnt-timber hills, watching the river water rush the bridge spiles, touching the grasshoppers that have turned black to blend in with the devastated environment. I'd need to be there to make sure I didn't get those details wrong.

Then you have no imagination. I couldn't have gotten the country in "River" and "Indian Camp" and "The End of Something" right if I'd been in Michigan because I'd only be recording them. By being far away I could picture those details like an impressionist painter, like Cézanne. I could give the pine scrub and heather a dreamy quality, a holy aura that's realer than real. Now take *To Have and Have Not*. That's my Key West book, and it's not as good as it should've been because I was in the Keys when I did it. I didn't have enough distance.

Q. But that's not true for *The Sun Also Rises*, is it? Part of its appeal is that it feels like it's being written as its actual events unfold. It's a *roman à clef,* a true-life novel whose names have been changed to protect the guilty.

The *roman à clef* controversy was a *roman à* crock. All reviewers could talk about was how the real Robert Cohn, Brett Ashley, and Mike Campbell were after me for exposing them as rummies and fornicators. By the way, I'll save you having to look up their real names, ladies and gentlemen—they were Harold Loeb, Duff Twysden, and Pat Guthrie.

James Joyce, Sylvia Beach, and Adrienne Monnier talk in Beach's Paris bookshop, Shakespeare and Company, a gathering spot for writers such as Ernest Hemingway.

Q. Yes, but didn't you once start a sequel in which your dramatis personae confront your narrator? Brett tells Jake Barnes about how tedious it is for her to be cornered in bars by tourists who congratulate her for starring in a notorious novel. Obviously, the line between fiction and fact was thin for you, too.

There you go again, discrediting the imagination.
The Sun has a lot more invented stuff than readers admit.
It was important for reviewers to say I just transcribed how

expatriates were *tromper*-ing each other because they wanted to believe I was celebrating young people going to pot. I wasn't. I wasn't encouraging anybody to come to Europe to get stewed. I was showing how my generation lacked rituals for making sense of the world.

Q. Regardless, *The Sun* made living abroad a fad. To this day, people carry it around Paris and Pamplona, searching for the same bars and restaurants. In a weird way many of them, college students especially, re-enact the book.

Yes, well, I haven't heard of too many students mangling themselves in homage to Jake Barnes, who can't love Brett because the war took away his genital abilities. That must mean students have some sense of when to throw the brake, huh? If they think *The Sun* glamorizes expatriate life they should look up stuff that's more straightforwardly critical of wastrels. I did an essay a few months after I came to France, "American Bohemians in Paris." "The scum of Greenwich Village, New York, has been skimmed off and deposited in large ladlesful on that section of Paris adjacent to the Café Rotonde." If that's not clear, get a seeing-eye dog.

Q. Yes, we forget that many Americans in Paris worked, especially the artists. It was the place to meet the modernist literati, whom you quickly became one of.

I wasn't the careerist Miss Stein later made me out to be. While I was lucky to be in the right place at the right time, I never felt like I was part of a movement, not even when my stories started appearing in *The Little Review*, the transatlantic review, *This Quarter*, and other "little magazines"

La Rotonde was a popular spot with the artistic crowd in 1922.

that expatriates all over Paris were starting. These were fly-by-night operations. They had a readership of maybe five, but they were five important readers who could make your name. Edmund Wilson was one—he reviewed my first two books, *Three Stories and Ten Poems* and *In Our Time*, when they had a combined circulation of 480 copies. But I never would've been successful if I hadn't had the goods. And it was in Paris that I got them. You know how, Mice? Hard work.

Q. That brings us to another important topic ...

5

THE HEMINGWAY STYLE

As early as 1927 critics hailed Hemingway as the most influential prose stylist of the era, his descriptive exactitude and taut rhythms making it impossible not to regard the genteel garrulity of Victorian writing as artificial and evasive. "Infectious" was another common description, for no sooner were dialogue, landscape description, and precise word choice identified as his trademark techniques than other writers began imitating them. Hemingway is so frequently parodied that today we forget just how experimental his style was. His patented techniques—most notably, his use of omission—introduced a new dramatic intensity into fiction.

Q. Your literary generation insisted that a writer's goal was to invent novel forms of expression. "Make it new!" Ezra Pound insisted, and, suddenly, how a story was told became more important than what the story was about. How did you discover your style?

I did it the way I describe myself doing it in *A Moveable Feast*—one sentence at a time. When I first came to Paris I rented a room on the Rue Descartes and wrote the six truest sentences I could: "If I started to write elaborately, or presenting something, I found that I could cut the scrollwork or ornament out and throw it away and start with the first true simple declarative sentence I had written." Once I did that, I realized that what you don't say says more than what you do. It was a short hop from that to my theory of omission, also known as my "iceberg principle."

Q. Can you remember the story in which you first used omission?

"Out of Season." I wrote it in 1923. Hadley and I were in Cortina, Italy. It was a literal transcription of an argument we had except that, as I later wrote in *Feast*, I "omitted the real end of it which was that the old man"—Peduzzi— "hanged himself."

Q. You know, I consider myself a pretty good reader, but "Out of Season" never made me think of suicide. To me it's always been about marriage.

That's why you don't read by theories, Mice. When I compared the effect of omission to an ice floe—"The dignity of movement of an iceberg is due to only one-eighth of it being above water"—I didn't intend for readers to go diving for that other seven-eighths. I was only saying that what's below the surface is still there even if you can't see it. The missing part may not be all that relevant. It wasn't in "Season" and I'm not so sure it was in "Big Two-Hearted River," although some professnorers have built careers trying to prove I wasn't joking when I said it was about coming back from the war only the war wasn't in it. Later I got so bored with them asking questions that I sent them chasing a red herring. I said that there were Indians in the story too

… and none of them appeared. That was a joke. Reading isn't meant to be a guessing game.

Q. I don't disagree in the case of "Out of Season," but in something like "Hills Like White Elephants" where the main conflict is only alluded to, isn't it the mystery of what's not explicit that engages the reader? In other words, isn't the interpretive task to figure out what you've omitted, if only for a basic understanding of what's going on?

Absolutely not. Crithacks want to classify "Hills Like White Elephants" as an abortion story because the word is never used. To classify it that way is to crassify it. It reduces drama to subject matter. The real interest in "Hills" is how the girl, Jig, and the American pressuring her to undergo the abortion talk to each other. Their back and forth is more important than what's making them go back and forth. It's a story about how men and women communicate— or how they don't communicate, that is, because they communicate so differently.

Q. OK, I can see that, but isn't the subject matter somewhat important? I mean, there seems to be a lot of fetal symbolism in the description of the landscape. Using a simile in the title seems a pretty blatant way of directing readers to it. They're led to wonder what exactly the hills of Spain's Ebro valley have to do with white elephants, and once they make the abortion connection, they associate the hills with Jig's unplanned pregnancy.

Here's a secret for you—all the symbolism that people talk about is crap. I used to get letters from students,

Dear Dr. Hemingstein, My English teacher says the sea in your book about it and that old man is really amniotic fluid. Could you confirm or deny? … Dear Comrade Hemingrrhoid, My professlurer says that Jake Barnes's genitals are defective and that this means moral eunuchs rule the world. Is that true? As I told George Plimpton, it's very bad for a writer to talk about how he writes. He writes to be read by the eye and no explanations or dissertations should be necessary. You can be sure that there's much more than will be read at any first reading and having made this it's not the writer's province to explain it or run guided tours through the more difficult country of his work. So if you want to believe the hills are alive with the sound of babies, you go right ahead. Just leave me out of it.

Q. Is there any other aspect of your writing besides symbolism that you thought critics overemphasized?

Dialogue. Around the time of *Men Without Women* the angleworms decided it was the only thing I was good at. They forgot about landscape, people, and so on and so on. *Vanity Fair* started it in 1928 with an unfunny piece about me using dialogue in the bullring instead of a cape. After that, you couldn't find a parodist that didn't make hay out of it.

Q. Is there a technique or device you used that you feel critics have neglected?

Stream of consciousness. I didn't invent it, of course. James Joyce didn't either, but he made it famous. The lit boys read "Hills" and "The Killers" and other stories, and they thought, "Here's an SOB who won't go into people's heads. He sticks to the outside, like a camera." They ignored how often I went inside.

I do it in the fourth chapter of *Green Hills of Africa*, which almost sounds like Faulkner, which is funny given how often I gave the shepherd's crook to Wild Bill Hiccup. I do it, too, at the end of *To Have and Have Not* when Harry Morgan's wife, Marie, has to confront his death—she's my Molly Bloom. And, of course, there are Harry Walden's dying visions of all the things he failed to write about in "The Snows of Kilimanjaro," and Robert Jordan's meditations on heroism in *For Whom the Bell Tolls*. So I fished the stream of consciousness and docked at the island of interior monologue a lot more than anyone ever recognized.

Q. Speaking of *For Whom the Bell Tolls*, you do something very controversial in the dialogue. The vote seems split as to whether it works.

You're talking about how the guerrillas say, "I obscenity in thy milk," and "Go unprintable yourself," right? Well, Spanish is the greatest language for profanity because it's so formal, and I couldn't do justice to the way the real Pilars and Pablos spoke if I let my publisher pepper the page with dashes, which is usually what happened when I tried to use blue words. I once took a copy of *A Farewell to Arms* and filled in the blanks: "No chance of -------. No place for ------." Not to shock you, Mr. Micey Mouse, but that's the way soldiers talk.

Q. I don't doubt it. But what gave you the idea in *For Whom* for translating curses that way? The technique is almost postmodern in the way it slaps back at censors who were forever trying to ban your work.

Hemingway saw bullfighting as an ethical contest between man and death.

There you go trying to crassify me again … but the idea came when I was escorting a pair of newspaperwomen around Madrid and our chauffeur swore up a hurricane when we blew a tire. The girls wanted to know what he was saying. They were both bugging me big time, but I couldn't figure out how to translate that talk into English without it losing its pique. Even if you could translate Spanish profanity, it wouldn't sound half as poetic. So I told the newspaperwomen, "He says expletive deleted in the unprintables of the gearshift of the car's mother," and I thought, "*Voilà!* That'll be a funny poke to all the censorship slobs." A lot of critics since then have guffawed at it. Even my wife at the time, Martha Gellhorn, thought it was silly.

Q. To me it's more effective than if you'd used the actual words. But that brings us to your reputation as a "dirty" writer. People today forget how much of your early notoriety had to do with your hells and SOBs. And those are just the ones you didn't have to replace with a dash.

The jerks never forgave me for believing a well-placed ---- is better than a mealy-mouthed copulation. It was bad enough when twits claimed I was a dirt hauler because I wrote about drinking and promiscuity. As late as the mid-'50s turd wrappers like *True* magazine were saying I "took obscene words off the backhouse wall and put them in print." This was after thirty years of my people having their mouths washed out with dashes. What nobody understood was that I never used obscenity for gratuitous shock. One should never use words which shock out of all proportion to their own value or connotation, I insisted, but nobody listened.

6

FICTION VS. NONFICTION

By the mid-1930s, Hemingway's reputation was in free fall thanks to his having abandoned the novel for nonfiction in *Death in the Afternoon* and *Green Hills of Africa*. Critics disparaged this shift, forgetting that Hemingway had begun his career as a journalist and that nonfiction, like war, was his way of keeping his writing grounded in the real world.

Q. What can writing journalism teach me?

It can teach you to avoid all the things that hamstrung Gertie S., Faulkner, Scott F., and Thomas Wolfe—mystification, maundering, and mooning. It can teach you to write a simple declarative sentence. But you have to get out of it fast.

Q. Why?

Because journalism is a racket. It puts a dollar value on your words that's destructive. You're writing to put food on the table, not art for art's sake. I never could've done the *In Our Time* stories if I hadn't quit the *Toronto Daily Star* in 1923.

Exposure to the war quickly provided Hemingway with experiences that otherwise might have taken a lifetime to acquire.

Hemingway disliked this staged publicity photo, lamenting, "I don't work like this."

Q. If that's the case, why did you take journalism up again in the 1930s? You covered the Spanish Civil War for the North American Newspaper Alliance in 1937–38, and you were the correspondent for *Collier's* during D-Day and the liberation of Paris in 1944.

I went back to news because it was the only way of getting close to those wars. Governments don't see much purpose in sending an artist to battle, but tell them you're a journalist, and they'll drive you to the front in a limousine.

Q. Most of your *Toronto* pieces from 1920 to '24 are feature writing, which is generally considered "soft" news. Critics have suggested that you were far better suited to this than the "hard" news of war reporting. They've been especially hard on your Spanish Civil War journalism, claiming you were "playing at war" and that you weren't objective because your anti-Fascism led you to ignore Communist atrocities. That's all from a book called *The First Casualty* by Philip Knightley, which is taught in introductory journalism classes.

Maybe Mr. Knighty-Knightley should go back to college himself. I was paid to go to Spain to write about myself going to Spain. Newspapers wanted my take on the situation, and that's what they got. They paid me as much as $1,000 a story when most reporters were getting $25.

Q. Your dispatches from Spain led directly to *For Whom the Bell Tolls*. In retrospect, do you think if you'd fictionalized *Death in the Afternoon* and *Green Hills of Africa*, they would have been better received? Many say that such stories as "The Undefeated" and "The Snows of Kilimanjaro" cover the same material but in a more compelling way.

I did nonfiction books because I had ideas I wanted to talk about, and if you write a novel of ideas, then the fiction goes to pot. I learned that from Tolstoy—I wrote that "*War and Peace* taught me to avoid 'big Political Thought passages,' which aren't as 'true and important and lasting' as the people." If you want to write fiction you have to show ideas through gestures rather than abstractions. But sometimes you want to think Big Thoughts, and that's what nonfiction's for.

Q. What Big Thoughts were you interested in?

How to write. That simple. Even though *Death* and *Green Hills* are about bullfighting and hunting, they're really about writing. I talk about what books are worth reading, why writers should avoid politics, and the elements of a good style. In *Death* I introduced my iceberg principle, and in *Green Hills* I defined the fourth and fifth dimension that prose writing should aim for. Those are concepts, and you can't get conceptual in fiction.

There's something else, too. I wanted to question whether nonfiction is all that different from fiction. There's fiction in both books, after all. I slipped an entire story, "A Natural History of the Dead," into *Death*, as well as an imaginary conversation with a reader who loathes bullfighting. In *Green Hills* I said my purpose was to write an absolutely true book,

Mary Welsh joined her husband on safari in Kenya in 1952.

but then I used fictitious names and novelistic techniques like stream of consciousness. Years later when I did *A Moveable Feast* I said, "If the reader prefers, this book may be regarded as fiction." The same holds for *Death* and *Green Hills*. There are always elements of fiction in nonfiction, and if your fiction is any good it'll have the ring of nonfiction, so—why must we label our literature, gentlemen?

7

ON FOOD, SPORT, AND RITUAL

H emingway frequently wrote about outdoor endeavors such as hunting, fishing, and, most famously, bullfighting. His works also describe countless meals—some exotic, some as plain as an onion sandwich, yet all depicted with ceremonial lavish. While detractors have been confounded by such seemingly minor fascinations, food and sport are integral to Hemingway's theme of moral engagement, for they are the rituals by which his heroes test their self-control in a world that encourages indulgence. At a time when values were growing increasingly relative, Hemingway viewed how one eats and plays as indices of the strength of character needed to steer clear of temptation.

Q. You've said that writing is like eating—that it's "not conscience, just peristaltic action." That's an unusual metaphor for writing. Can you explain it?

I used that term because peristalsis is the muscular process that's central to digesting. The key word is process. Pick any of the things I wrote about and what you'll find is an outline of their process.

Eating and drinking are ways to learn self-control, according to Hemingway.

Mary Welsh joined her husband and friends, including actor Spencer Tracy (on Hemingway's right), at *La Floridita* bar in Havana, Cuba.

Q. Can you give me an example?

Choose any you'd like—eating, fishing, bullfighting, hunting, yencing—making love … well, no, I never got that specific with the yencing. It's easiest to see in bullfighting because appreciating it requires a technical understanding of its traditions. In *Death in the Afternoon* I called the process the "certain definite action." Living is the act of sussing out rules by testing them, so it's only natural that I wrote about processing experience by describing the specific steps for surviving heroically. From the minute I saw my first *corrida* in 1923 I recognized that bullfighting is an ethical contest between man and death and that its rules of engagement provide a graceful, aesthetic analogy to confronting the violence of being.

Hemingway, shown with Antonio Ordonez in 1960, loved bullfighting from the time of his first *corrida* in 1923.

Fly-fishing at Walloon Lake provided Hemingway with material for short stories.

Now there are matador characters who meet this challenge and others who cheat it—Juan Belmonte in *The Sun*, for example. Belmonte lost his sense of reality by demanding too many safeguards, and the crowd knew he was faking. Niño de la Palma was another. He inspired Pedro Romero, but I no sooner wrote *The Sun* than Niño was gored and went phooey with fear. I described his nerved-up performances in *Death* as "the brave actions of a coward."

Q. Curiously, you write as often about the ethics of watching the bullfight as of performing it.

There's a right way to follow it, too. In *The Sun* I called this *afición*—"passion." When you're passionate about bullfighting, you're not concerned with spectacle but with expertise—you understand the knowledge that makes it an art form, and you appreciate the training behind that artistry. An aficionado is dedicated to preserving that expertise. Unfortunately, Jake Barnes breaks the aficionado code by introducing Pedro to Brett Ashley, who seduces and corrupts the boy. Jake loses his standing among the bullfight insiders thanks to Brett and the other drunken expatriates.

Q. How does the "certain definite action" relate to hunting and fishing? Confronting mortality doesn't seem as evident in them.

Come on safari and let me hear you say you don't face death hunting. If you can't, do the next best thing and read "The Short Happy Life of Francis Macomber." That's about a coward earning his cojones back after bolting from a charging lion. He's just about to earn them, too, when his bloody wife blows his head off—whether by accident or design is for you to decide.

Even when mortality isn't at stake, how people hunt reveals their morality. *Green Hills of Africa* is me learning that. Through the safari, Papa struggles to not be competitive and braggadocious, those very faults the bastards said I never admitted in print. In the end I come out humbled but respectful of the code.

It's in the fishing stuff, too. Read "Big Two-Hearted River," in which Nick Adams fishes to discover his place in nature. The entire trip is a test. Will he reel in his fish without rushing and breaking the line? Will he spoil the dinner his hiking all day has earned him by eating too fast and burning his tongue? Will he remember not to touch the trout he won't keep with a dry hand so they won't die of fungus? As Nick learns, every single action has consequences. That's the moral of my work.

Q. Interestingly, whenever you write about these rituals, you draw analogies to writing. "River" originally ended with Nick meditating on literary ethics, not fishing.

Writing's a ritual, too. You're still learning the "certain definite action." Read *The Garden of Eden*. David's trying to take shelter from his crumbling marriage in the sanctity of a good sentence. Read *A Moveable Feast*—that's me learning the definite action. It's all the same thing, Mice—the bullfight, the hunt, the river, the sentence. These are the things you must master to make it in a world that's out to break you.

Hemingway—seen here hunting with actor Gary Cooper in
Sun Valley, Idaho—struggled with his celebrity.

8

ON FEUDS AND RIVALRIES

lthough he owed significant debts to Gertrude Stein, F. Scott Fitzgerald, and many others, Hemingway bristled at any suggestion that his writing was shaped anywhere but in the crucible of his own literary convictions. His irritation led him to renounce the influence of mentors and peers, often in violent language, such as his professed desire in 1924 to run T.S. Eliot through a meat grinder. *A Moveable Feast* provided a later opportunity to settle perceived scores and ridicule Stein's lesbianism, Fitzgerald's alcoholism, and John Dos Passos's illegitimate birth. Such hostility has inspired much speculation about Hemingway's thin skin and inveterate competitiveness.

Q. When *In Our Time* was published, reviewers declared you the "offspring" of Sherwood Anderson and Gertrude Stein. Was that irritating?

It annoyed me because it wasn't true. In 1922 I did one story, "My Old Man," that sounded like Sherwood, and suddenly I'm the fruit of his loins. The danger of having famous friends is that readers hear their voices in yours. That's why, from the 1930s on, Your Author preferred a non-literary

Writer and journalist John Dos Passos became a target of his former friend.

crowd. It's better when only one writer is in the room and best when you're it. Now, name me something besides "My Old Man" that sounds like old Sherwon't.

Q. Well, there's *The Torrents of Spring*, of course, but that's a parody done to declare your independence from him. Do you regret doing such a hatchet job on Anderson? He introduced you to Gertrude Stein, after all.

I don't recommend devoting a whole book to telling a bastard he's gone dry. I later apologized: "I did *Torrents* because I was righteous, which is the worst thing you can be … It was cruel and I was an SOB to do it."

Q. The apology was about thirty-five years late, though, wasn't it? You wrote that in 1959. Anderson had been dead for nearly twenty years.

Being a friend and being honest aren't the same things. Tell a writer he's great when you know he's faking and you're a phony yourself. Shoot straight and you're an ungenerous jerk. Frankly, I'd rather be a jerk. Friends are a dime a dozen, but good writing is rare.

Q. What did you learn from Gertrude Stein?

I learned repetition, rhythm, and landscape. I never denied what she taught me, not even after she came after me in *The Autobiography of Alice B. Toklas*. I took what I needed from her and moved on, though nobody recognized it. As late as 1934 guys like Wyndham Lewis were still grousing about "the steining of Hemingway." That's not the gen. When I went to Gertrude's I wasn't wined, dined, or steined.

F. Scott Fitzgerald was criticized in Hemingway's "The Snows of Kilimanjaro."

Her rhythms are centrifugal, but mine are centripetal. If mine were like hers, I'd never have been able to omit things. Read *The Making of Americans* and you'll see that Gertrude couldn't leave anything out—anything, that is, except the truth.

Q. You were also notoriously hard on F. Scott Fitzgerald. You ridiculed him as a sycophant in "The Snows of Kilimanjaro" and in *A Moveable Feast* as an irresponsible drunk. Did you ever feel you'd been too callous?

Scott and I had a lot in common. We were both Midwesterners revolting against the genteelorrhea of Midwestern values, but neither of us could stomach bohemians. We believed in hard work, love, and discipline, but we had different attitudes about whether they were achievable. Scott idealized failure. That was his inferiority complex, and it made him easy prey.

"A Matter of Measurements" is the *Feast* chapter you're talking about. You see it as ridicule, but really, I was doing Fitz a favor. I was building his confidence. You've got to believe you're the most manly guy in the room if you want to be a great writer.

Q. Your friend Donald Ogden Stewart—the inspiration for Bill Gordon in *The Sun*—once said that the minute you were beholden to somebody, his days in your circle were numbered: "I think it was a psychological fear he had that you might ask something from him. He didn't want to be overdrawn at your bank." Do you think that's accurate?

Beetle dung. I'll tell you what I once said: "The most essential gift for a good writer is a built-in, shockproof,

BS detector." Honest criticism you can trust is how you calibrate that apparatus, and that's what good friends give you. I admit my luck in having them. I had Gertrude to tell me that "remarks are not literature" and so I chopped off the rambling ending of "Big Two-Hearted River." Scott was there in June 1926 to convince me that the opening chapter of *The Sun* was full of "elephantine facetiousness." That's the kind of marble-mouth word he liked, but he was right, so I lopped off the first sixteen pages and the book was stronger. Later there was John Dos Passos telling me to cut the preachier parts of *Death in the Afternoon*.

This input is valuable, but you also learn that friends aren't always right, and you have to know when they've cheated you with bad advice. Gertrude was wrong about "Up in Michigan" being inaccrochable—unfit for public viewing. Virtually everything Scott said when he sent me a nine-page critique of *A Farewell to Arms* was screwy, so I wrote "Kiss My Ass" on his letter and filed it away. Old Dos was rarely right. I still remember him reviewing *The Sun* and calling it a "cock and bull story about a lot of summer tourists getting drunk." This from someone who couldn't invent people if his one good eye depended on it.

If you want to know why I broke with friends, it's very simple: after a while, they had nothing more to teach me.

Q. In the end, there were only two literary relationships that you didn't abruptly terminate— Ezra Pound and Maxwell Perkins.

I almost ended it with Ezra before the friendship really began. He was an affected sort and when I first got to Paris I caricatured him for *The Little Review*. If Lewis Galantière

Maxwell Perkins served as editor to both Ernest Hemingway and F. Scott Fitzgerald.

hadn't talked me out of publishing that parody, Ez's ire would've had his Van Dyke spontaneously combusting and he wouldn't have published my first little book, *Three Stories and Ten Poems*. I knew he and Your Author could get along when he asked me to teach him to box. He asked me, see? Gertrude learned from me, too—she copied my dialogue— but not only couldn't she ask, she couldn't admit, either.

Q. What about Maxwell Perkins? Thanks to you and Fitzgerald he's the most famous editor in literary history, and yet he seems to have served completely different roles for his authors.

Max was the best editor a writer could have because he only offered as many suggestions as you asked for. Because Scott had no confidence, Max was his handmaiden. Because Thomas Wolfe couldn't put a damned story together to save his thyroid gland, Max was his midwife. With me all he had to do was be a friend, and he was a fine one. He never asked me to change anything I wrote except to remove certain words which were not then publishable … For me he was not an editor.

Keep in mind he didn't always think my stuff was perfect. We disagreed over *A Farewell to Arms*. He never thought the war and love stories came together in the end. He said that after Frederic and Catherine make it to Switzerland, the war's forgotten, and he wanted Catherine's death linked to it. How the Italian retreat from Caporetto can bloody cause a Caesarean section is beyond me, and I lost my temper. I was so embarrassed by the foul things I said that I asked Max to destroy the letter I said them in—which he did. That was Max. He was wrong about the ending, but I was wrong about getting foul with him.

9

ON WIVES

Hemingway's tangled marital history suggests that he was an unrepentant womanizer. Such a reputation does a great disservice both to him and to his four wives, all of whom were central influences. Hadley Richardson, Pauline Pfeiffer, Martha Gellhorn, and Mary Welsh were strong, talented women in their own right, in many ways more complex and more interesting than the fictional heroines they inspired. Ultimately, the dissolution of each relationship bespeaks Hemingway's inability to sustain lasting emotional ties—a failing he both admitted and lamented when depicting isolated men defeated by the complexities of love.

Q. You relied heavily on your wives for literary advice. Would you consider them collaborators?

That's your word, not mine. I never borrowed from their diaries or letters like Scott did. None of them added words or phrases in the margins like Alice did for Gertrude. Mainly they told me when I was going phony, and they let me work. Being married to a writer isn't easy. Your wife has to understand that when you're not working you're feeling lousy. She can't distract. That was Scott's problem—Zelda was jealous of Scott's work. He'd start to work and as soon as he

Pauline Pfeiffer, Hemingway's second wife, was wealthier and more worldly than his first wife, Hadley.

was working well, Zelda would get bored and take him off to another drunken party. I may have had four wives, but none of them ever did that to me.

Q. They also have to understand the difference between fiction and a writer's real feelings. It couldn't have been easy on your first wife, Hadley, to be pregnant in 1923 and to read stories about young men dreading the emotional entanglements of marriage and fatherhood.

You're thinking of "Cross Country Snow," in which Nick tries to convince his friend George he's excited about being a father, or the cut part of "Big Two-Hearted River," in which Nick laments all the friends he lost after he married. I put it more harshly in "The Three-Day Blow"—"Once a man's married he's absolutely bitched."

What people don't understand is that I was going for the tragedy of this feeling. I wasn't being anti-woman. I was saying that men want to love every bit as much as women, but they're afraid of complications, and love is always complicating. I said it best in *Green Hills*. Men "do not want to be lonesome. They are afraid to be alone in their beliefs and no woman would love any of them enough so that they could kill their lonesomeness in a woman, or pool it with hers, or make something with her that makes the rest of it unimportant." The problem of being a man is how you handle the complications even when you've a bad habit of daydreaming about escaping them. The only thing escaping gets you is lonesomeness, and that's no escape.

Q. After your divorce from Hadley, you expressed great sorrow over leaving her for Pauline Pfeiffer,

your second wife. That couldn't have been easy for Pauline. More than any of your wives your writing snipes at her. In "The Snows of Kilimanjaro," Harry takes out his self-hatred on his "rich bitch" wife, blaming his corruption on her family's money. It strikes readers as a little ungrateful considering the Pfeiffer family paid $33,000 to send you on the African safari that inspired that story.

Don't forget to mention that's $33,000 in the heart of the Depression. All the biographers do that, just to emphasize how lousy of a lout I was to Pauline. No, it's true, she didn't get her literary due. See, no matter how much you go on to love in life, you always remember the first one because she was there before you were yourself, and you remember all the possibilities of who you might have become. With a second love that starts in adultery like mine and Pauline's did you always feel guilty. First you're a couple and then you're a couple with an unmarried friend and suddenly you're a husband, with two attractive girls around, and if you have bad luck you get to love them both.

Q. You're quoting from *A Moveable Feast*, which portrays Pauline as "unrelentingly" set on stealing you from Hadley. It's telling that you don't even use Pauline's name in that book—she's the "unmarried young woman" and the "temporary best friend."

Parts of *Feast* about Pauline never made it into print. I said I never worked better nor was I happier than with her. That was left out because it was a beginning, not an ending, and I was saving it for a later memoir about love, remorse, contrition, and unbelievable happiness and the story of truly good work and final sorrow. If you want a taste of that "unbelievable happiness," read *Green Hills of Africa*. I call Pauline P.O.M., or "Poor Old Mama," and it's a very full and happy picture of our love.

Q. If you were so happy, why did you begin an affair with Martha Gellhorn in 1936? Friends said you needed a new love to write your next "big" book. You had to leave Hadley after *The Sun Also Rises* and have Pauline to do *A Farewell to Arms*, and now you had to leave Pauline and have Martha to do *For Whom the Bell Tolls*.

Real friends don't theorize. I fell for Marty because she was a writer herself, and she lived to travel, and most of all because she was political. I'd gotten fat in Key West, and I needed my vitality back. The best part of Marty wasn't the marriage. It was being in Madrid with her in '37 and '38 during the Spanish Civil War. We had a fine extramarital time at the Hotel Florida, making love and dodging Generalissimo Franco's shells.

If you don't believe I felt bad, read my play, *The Fifth Column*. There's a line in which a whore tells the hero, Philip Rawlings, not to get kinked up with Dorothy Bridges. "I want to make an absolutely colossal mistake," he says. That's how I felt, and that's what I did.

Q. You both made a mistake. *The Fifth Column* is disturbing for its negative portrait of Dorothy, whom you describe as a "bored Vassar bitch" and a "lazy" writer. Folks have wondered why Ms. Gellhorn didn't leave you on the spot.

The play was my way of pushing her to leave me. Rawlings and Dorothy don't marry, you see. But Marty never complained about *The Fifth Column*. She took it as a joke.

Q. Popular perception is that your third marriage didn't last because of rivalry, that you felt Martha was more committed to journalism than to you, especially after 1942, when she was reporting full-time on World War II.

For God's sake, don't quote that telegram: Are You a War Correspondent or a Wife in My Bed? I regretted it the minute I sent it, knowing I'd spend eternity with biogassers citing it back at me. The rivalry wasn't one-sided. Every time Marty put out a book, she was compared to her Heminghubby. And Your Author took the blame for that marriage. Read *Across the River and Into the Trees*. "You lose women the same way you lose a battalion; by errors of judgment, orders that are impossible to fill, and through impossible conditions. And through brutality."

Q. Your final marriage to Mary Welsh was your longest—fifteen years, as opposed to thirteen with Pauline and five each with Hadley and Martha. Yet it doesn't excite as much interest as the others.

That's because I wasn't publishing much fiction with Mary. I was writing a lot—*Islands in the Stream*, *The Garden of Eden*, and the Africa book—but I only put out two novels, *Across the River and Into the Trees* and *The Old Man and the Sea*. Miss Mary wasn't in either of them, and readers only want to know your wife when you make her a character.

Q. For better or worse, her main literary contribution seems to be the sexual experimentation you explore

in *Garden*. **When a portion of that manuscript was published in 1986, people were shocked by the role swapping between David and Catherine Bourne. It excited some rather prurient curiosity about your sex life with Mary.**

Another example of how biography is buggery. I wrote an entry in Miss Mary's diary remembering a time in Torcello, Italy. "Mary has never had one lesbian impulse but has always wanted to be a boy … I loved feeling the embrace of Mary which came to me as something quite new and outside all tribal law. On the night of December 19th we worked out these things and I have never been happier." From the way the hackademics have latched on to that passage, you'd think I'd written *Lady Chatterley's Lover*.

Q. Well, I think scholars are trying to do you the favor of understanding your obsession with manliness by saying that those erotic experiments make your thinking on sex and gender more complicated than what the macho stereotype suggests.

If you want to understand what happened in my marriages, re-read "In Another Country." It was never about sex. It was always about love and loss. The Italian major tells Nick he must never marry because he's bitter over his wife dying of pneumonia: "If a man is to lose everything, he should not place himself in a position to lose anything. He should not place himself in a position to lose. He should find things he cannot lose." If I made one mistake with my wives it's that I put myself in a position to lose, but unlike the major, it was a loss of my own making. You see, I never made myself believe I couldn't lose Hash and Mama and Marty and Miss Mary.

Mary Welsh and Hemingway lived in Cuba during the early years of their marriage.

You have to be absolutely convinced you can't live without the one you love, and I never did and I paid the price … so let's move on, can we?

10

ON FEMALE CHARACTERS

onventional wisdom insists that realistic females are rare in Hemingway's writing. His typical heroine, detractors complain, is either compliant and submissive or an emasculating **harridan**. However, accusations of chauvinism are misplaced. In their rush to condemn Hemingway, critics fail to appreciate the nuances of Catherine Barkley in *A Farewell to Arms* or Maria in *For Whom the Bell Tolls*. Recently, defenders have begun to demonstrate how such characters exemplify the same heroic qualities as their male counterparts. Such efforts have gone a long way toward redressing Hemingway's reputation for misogyny.

Q. There's a perception out there that you were better at basing female characters on women you knew instead of inventing them. People point to the difference between, say, the sensitive wife in "Cat in the Rain" (based on Hadley) and Marie Morgan in *To Have and Have Not*.

My people were never literal translations of women I knew. Readers assume Catherine Barkley was Agnes von Kurowsky, but Ag herself never saw the resemblance. In truth, Catherine was part Ag, part Hadley, with some Pauline,

Actress Ingrid Bergman (left) joined Hemingway and Martha Gellhorn to discuss the lead role in *For Whom the Bell Tolls.*

and even a little of Duff Twysden's Britishness left over from Brett in *The Sun*. What's your problem with Marie Morgan, anyway?

Q. Well, she hardly seems a genuine portrait of working-class womanhood. Her husband, Harry, loses his arm, but all Marie can talk about is how sexually stimulating she finds his new "stump." Even for your ardent fans their lovemaking scene is a bit … embarrassing.

You sound like the idiotlogues that came after me in the 1930s. They only liked proletarian women when they were baring their breasts to feed malnourished men—*Grapes of Wrath* gals, in other words. Who's doing the stereotyping now? Marie's comforting her husband in that scene, you dope. She's assuring Harry he's still a man even though he's maimed.

Q. That's an interesting defense, but how about the perception that your attitude toward women hardened after your divorce from Hadley?

I see where this is going. You're saying, "Listen, Hymenstein, with Brett you showed how a woman goes tragic by expressing her need for love through promiscuity, but then you go create what could have been a similar character with Helène Bradley in *To Have* and all you can do is call her a bitch."

Ignore *To Have and Have Not*—at least the parts that aren't about Harry and Marie. The rest is a botch. Helène Bradley was supposed to show what a tragedy it is for a woman to get caught in a loveless marriage, but I couldn't say what I wanted to because I'd based Helène and her husband, Tommy, on Jane and Grant Mason, friends of mine from Cuba, and the portrait was libelous. That's the writer's predicament—you want to show the real sorrow in somebody's situation but you've got to worry about lawsuits. If I hardened after Hadley, it was because I hated lawyers, not women.

Q. Did you ever regret calling your second story collection *Men Without Women*? Some see the title as a taunt—it almost challenges people not to view you as anti-female.

What I regret is how Scribner's advertised the title. Max Perkins took a line without asking from a letter in which I said the softening feminine influence is absent in my stories either through training, discipline, death, or situation. A lot of women, Virginia Woolf included, came after me for that.

Q. That's ironic given that *Men Without Women*'s most famous story is "Hills Like White Elephants," which many consider your most sympathetic portrait of a woman.

They say that about Jig because the American who wants her to have an abortion is so obviously a crut. That's clear villainy. I happen to think I did much better women elsewhere—Catherine in *Arms*, for example. Reviewers complained she was too romanticized. Hell, even Fitz said that. What they didn't get was that Catherine was romanticizing herself. She's trying to escape the war by assuming the trappings of courtly love. The slightly formal way she talks is supposed to clue you to that. I knew it wasn't real—that was my point. For both Frederic and her, idealizing love is a survival mechanism.

Q. Is that also true for Maria in *For Whom the Bell Tolls*?

It's very true. The critpricks couldn't believe that a woman so recently gang-raped by Fascists could find her way into an American's sleeping bag, but Robert Jordan is Maria's way of overcoming her trauma. Choosing to love is her taking control of her life from the SOBs who violated her.

Here's what I don't get, Mice. They knock me for being macho, but when I do a sincere love story, I'm ridiculed. You know, of course, that the most mocked line I ever wrote is from *For Whom*: "Did thee feel the earth move?" That's what Robert Jordan says after he and Maria make love. People assume he wants acknowledgment of what a great lover he is, but really he wants some assurance that their union is spiritual and transcendent. I wanted the lovers' dialogue to sound like metaphysical poetry, which was not inappropriate for a book whose title and epigraph come from John Donne. A spiritual union is all Robert and Maria have to endure war.

Q. Your third most controversial heroine is probably Catherine Bourne in *The Garden of Eden*. She seems to pay the price for her unconventional sexuality by going insane. The fact that her husband, David, "cures" Catherine's bisexual lover, Marita, of her lesbian tendencies likewise suggests that the book endorses conventional heterosexual roles.

I don't endorse or enforce anything. I show people in the thick of what they're going through. Catherine and David have a very adventurous love life at first, but the role reversals scare him. Games are exciting but when a man faces the prospect of losing power permanently in a relationship he's going to revert to simple beliefs, and there's no simpler one than the idea that men are men and women are women.

That's the tragedy for David. He can't give up being the man. That's the point, not that he should be the man. If there's a problem with how that idea gets conveyed, it's because too much of the story is narrated through David's perspective. There are unpublished parts that let the reader sympathize more with Catherine and Marita, but they didn't make it into the final book. If I'd had the guts to put *Eden* out when I was writing it, nobody would've ever accused me of machismo.

Q. Let's imagine a woman averse to reading you because of your reputation. How would you encourage her to overcome that prejudice?

I'd say, "If you don't like me, dear reader, put your finger over the header where it says By Ernest Hemingway and pretend you're reading someone else. You'll hear voices that don't sound a whit like you think I sound." Even better, I'd say pretend you're not reading anybody. You'll be surprised, I promise. You'll discover that my Catherines and Marias and Maritas gain dimension and come to life when they're no longer thought of as my creations. The great thing about people is that they can be read in many different and contradictory ways. When you hear them through the lips of the writer, though, you only hear what you think the writer is saying. The truth, as always, is more complicated.

11

THE PRICE OF FAME

W hile the 1940s and '50s were years of artistic decline for Hemingway, they conversely mark the apex of his fame. Interestingly, commentators often attribute his downward spiral to his celebrity as much as to alcoholism and depression. As one recent reviewer glibly remarks, "Ernest Hemingway was the first American celebrity writer, and it probably killed him." Such assertions imply that Hemingway could have sustained his art had he simply avoided the spotlight, a claim that ignores the audience's non-literary desire to revere and emulate media heroes.

Q. When were you first aware of your celebrity?

I always had a talent for attracting publicity. I was no sooner off the ship after World War I than the *New York Sun* wanted a dockside interview with the first American wounded in Italy. I was page eight news there, and page three in the *Chicago American*—Worst Shot-up Man In U.S. on Way Home.

Real celebrity didn't start until 1929, though. There was some early press in the *In Our Time* years, but they were about me being a writer and not about me being me. Then suddenly I'm in Paris boxing at the American Club with

Hemingway met his first love, Agnes von Kurowsky (center), while recovering from his war wounds.

a journalist named Morley Callaghan with Fitz keeping time on our one-minute rounds. Only Scott is lousy at timekeeping and he lets a round go four minutes, at which point Your Author has sustained several shots to the kisser and is going down. Lo and behold, the story makes the papers. Callaghan KOs Hemingstiff! It was the tone that taught me what celebrity is about—it's about debunking you. The press wants to show that Papa's not the man he says he is if another man can draw blood first ...

It doesn't take thirty years of that speculation to start wondering if they're right. It happens when you realize you're acting like yourself to prove the press wrong. Then, when they still doubt you, you find yourself exaggerating who you are, and by then, it's really too late, and you're a damned cartoon.

Q. Why didn't you just change your public image if you felt forced to live up to it?

Do that and you're admitting you've been pulling the wool over the public the entire time. And that's when they really turn on you. Every interview, every photograph, every personality profile had to authenticate your image, even when the facts were cockeyed.

"Here, Hem," the press boys would say, "sit next to this dead lion so we can snap one for *Life*—we know you didn't shoot the bugger, but we know you could have. So what if it's not the gen?" … "Hey, Hem, let us *Town & Country* saps describe you working in your study. What's that? You're black ass and on the block right now because we're looking over your shoulder? Who cares? Just pretend!"

There was only one time I tried to change my image, and it blew up like a trench mortar.

Q. Let me guess—Lillian Ross's 1950 *New Yorker* profile. People still argue over whether she was mocking you.

She wasn't. I was mocking me—the legend of me, anyway. I was tossing manure about socking Dostoevsky and Tolstoy, making up stories, talking punch-drunk, but everybody took it seriously. Readers wanted the "real" Hem, but sometimes I get so tired of sounding like me that I invent ways of not sounding like me. Lillian didn't know I was pulling her leg, and the next thing I know the press is calling me a deluded coot.

Q. One thing that profile painfully exposes is your heavy alcohol consumption. There are photos galore

of you inebriated in the 1950s. Given the press' emphasis on "boozing," do you ever wish you'd been a bit more discreet about drinking?

My generation grew up drinking behind closed doors. By the time we'd lived through twelve years of Prohibition, we'd earned the right to do it in public. I wouldn't trust a man I couldn't see drunk.

Q. All I'm saying is that alcohol not only impinged on your output but negatively affected perceptions of you. "Boozing" is one of those things that people who've never read you think they know about you.

Don't diagnose me! Anybody who says I reveled in rummyhood hasn't read my books. Drinking's a discipline—that's what Jake forgets in *The Sun* and it's why he ruins Pamplona for himself. Maybe I didn't have that discipline myself but I created people who tried to gain it. Next subject, please.

Q. OK ... Did you ever have second thoughts about writing for slicks like *Life*, *Holiday*, and *Look* in the 1950s? Articles such as "The Great Blue River" and "The Dangerous Summer" seemed to damage your literary reputation, with critics dismissing them as image management rather than art.

The crityaks were jealous. *Life* paid $90,000 for "The Dangerous Summer." I deserved the money after giving so much for so long. These pieces weren't supposed to be part of "the reputation." I was writing for a different audience. Some readers desired the simple, pleasant Papa, and for $90,000 I was happy to give it to them. If those articles aren't up

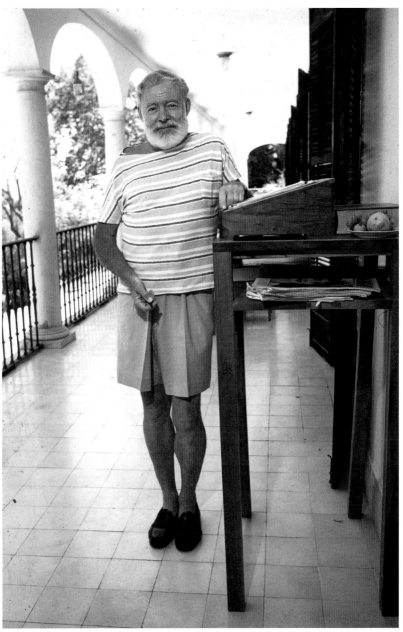

Hemingway used this standing desk when writing "The Dangerous Summer."

to standards, gentlemen, go seek out *A Moveable Feast* and you'll have the Hemingway you want.

Q. Is there anything final you'd like to say?

Only that if we could have made this enough of a dialogue, it would've had everything in it that matters—everything about the writing, that is. It would have the clicking oarlocks of the canoes in "Indian Camp" and the limestone foundation of the deserted sawmill in "The End of Something" and the whap of the blackjack on Ad Francis's skull in "The Battler." It would have the acetylene flares on the Avenue des Gobelins that Jake and Brett notice in *The Sun Also Rises* and the way Ole Andreson's feet hang over the end of his bed in "The Killers." It would include the ants trying to escape the burning log in *A Farewell to Arms* and the old man's stack of brandy saucers in "A Clean, Well-Lighted Place." It would have the dry smell of heather in *For Whom the Bell Tolls* and the slosh of the shark waters in *The Old Man and the Sea.* It would have the seal skins you attached to the bottom of the skis to climb the funicular-less slopes in Schruns in *A Moveable Feast*, and it would have so much more, too, because there was so much more …

It would have every detail that I worked hard to pack into every sentence, and work's the word I want you to walk away with—not personality, not fame, not reputation, not Paris nor Papa nor Papa dobles at the Floridita nor a shotgun barrel on a summer Ketchum morning when there was finally peace after so much pain. The only thing that matters is the work. The pleasure of doing it well was the only reason I ever wanted to write, and it's a pleasure I look forward to

(From left to right) Ernest Hemingway and his wife Mary Welsh at the Stork Club for a celebrity dinner featuring Nancy Hawkes, actors Spencer Tracy and George Jessel, and producer Leland Hayward (1950).

feeling in the seconds after you leave me when I'll press this pencil to this paper and if I'm lucky I'll have earned the right to smile and say, Yes, yes, old Hem, you've poured difficult emotions into a fine and durable sentence but now there's the next one to do so don't get too content. There is and always will be work to do.

Still, there's no greater satisfaction than finishing a good sentence, Mice. Remember that if you remember nothing else.

GLOSSARY

abhorrence: A feeling of repulsion.

avant-garde: A group that develops new or experimental concepts, especially in the arts.

bequeath: Leave something to a person or other beneficiary by a will.

enigmatic: Difficult to interpret or understand; mysterious.

ethos: Guiding beliefs of a person, group or organization.

existential: Relating to or affirming existence.

harridan: A strict, bossy, or belligerent old woman.

hedonism: Doctrine that pleasure and happiness are the most important goals in life.

intuit: Understand or work out by instinct.

le bon mot: A clever remark; literally "the good word."

machismo: An exaggerated masculinity and an exhilarating sense of power and strength.

misogyny: A hatred of women.

modernism: A breaking away from Victorian conventions; in writing, it is a style seeking to change literary convention and "make it new."

Montparnasse: A neighborhood in Paris on the Left Bank known in the 1920s and '30s as the center of the intellectual and artistic life of the city.

paean: A song of praise or triumph.

Rabelaisian: Displaying earthy or bawdy humor.

Rorschach: A personality and intelligence test in which a subject interprets inkblot designs in terms that reveal intellectual and emotional factors.

scrupulous: Thorough and extremely attentive to details.

slicks: A magazine printed on glossy or high quality paper.

stoicism: Enduring pain or hardship without showing emotion or complaining.

truculence: Defiant aggressiveness.

viscerally: Coming from strong emotions and not reason.

For FURTHER INFORMATION

Books

DeFazio, Albert J. III, Sandra Spanier, and Robert W. Trogdon, eds. *The Letters of Ernest Hemingway, Volume 2, 1923–1925*. Cambridge, England: Cambridge University Press, 2013.

Lyons, Nick, ed. *Hemingway on Fishing*. New York, NY: Scribner, 2002.

McLain, Paula. *The Paris Wife*. New York, NY: Random House, 2011.

Phillips, Larry W., ed. *Hemingway on Writing*. New York, NY: Scribner, 1999.

Reynolds, Michael. *Hemingway: The Paris Years*. New York, NY: W.W. Norton Company, 1999.

Spanier, Sandra, and Robert W. Trogdon, eds. *The Letters of Ernest Hemingway, Volume 1, 1907–1922*. Cambridge, England: Cambridge University Press, 2011.

Website

www.theparisreview.org/interviews/4825/the-art-of-fiction-no-21-ernest-hemingway

Writer George Plimpton's interview with Ernest Hemingway for the *Paris Review* in a story titled "The Art of Fiction."

INDEX

ABOUT *the* AUTHOR

Kirk Curnutt has written thirteen volumes of fiction and literary criticism, including several about Ernest Hemingway and F. Scott Fitzgerald. His first novel, *Breathing Out the Ghost*, won the 2008 Best Books of Indiana competition in the fiction category and was a *Foreword Magazine* Book of the Year finalist. He is a professor and chair of English at Troy University's Montgomery Campus in Montgomery, Alabama, and serves as a director of the Alabama Book Festival. He was the recipient of a 2007-08 Alabama State Arts Council literary fellowship.

John Updike is a novelist who won Pulitzer Prizes for fiction for *Rabbit is Rich* (1981) and *Rabbit at Rest* (1991). At the age of thirty-two, he became the youngest person ever elected to the National Institute of Arts and Letters. He received the National Medal of Art from President George H.W. Bush in 1989, and in 2003 was presented with the National Medal for the Humanities from President George W. Bush. He died in 2009 from lung cancer.